Richard Tyrone Jones was born in 1980 in the West Midlands. He read History at King's College, Cambridge and now travels the UK as a writer, educator, performer, live literature promoter and host of the popular 'Utter!' spoken word events, writing workshops and MisGuided tours. His work has been published in many magazines and periodicals and he has read for most of the UK's major live poetry series. Since 2010 he has been Director of Spoken Word at Edinburgh's Free Fringe (**freefringe.org.uk**). Also in that year, his own heart almost killed him, but at least he got a show out of it. This is the book of that show, with special additional material.

www.richardtyronejones.com

Richard Tyrone Jones's Big Heart

(and other complications)

Richard Tyrone Jones's Big Heart
(and other complications)

Copyright Richard Tyrone Jones 2012

The right of Richard Tyrone Jones to be identified as the author of this work has been asserted in accordance with the Copyright, Designs and Patents Acts 1988.

ISBN: 978 – 1 – 909211 – 00 – 1

A CIP record for this title is available from the British Library.

Published by **www.allographic.co.uk.** An allographic / **www.utterspokenword.com** co-production. Cover photos by Andrew Crowe. Interior art by patternfightperformance.

Printed in Cambria, Constantia, and (briefly) Comic Sans MS in the UK by bookprintinguk.com.

Some of these pieces have previously appeared in *Nasty Little Press Ration Book, New Trespass, Rising* and *Tales of the Decongested Vol II.* Thanks to their editors.

Richard is on twitter: @rtjpoet, at richardtyronejones.com and richardtyronejones@gmail.com.

Case history

Prognosis

What becomes of the broken-hearted?

Complications (extra material)

Foreword

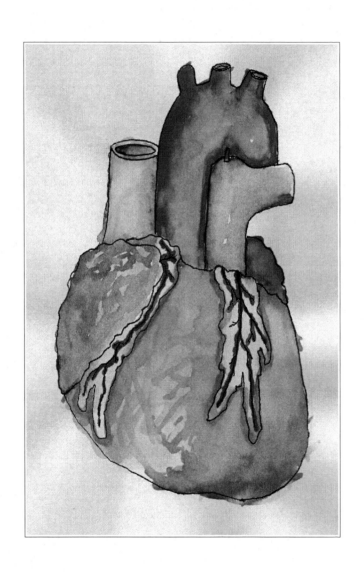

Foreword

Dearest reader. Thank you for buying this book. Hope you enjoyed the show. If you haven't seen the show, please see the show. If you love the book, it's just like the book, only coming out of my face.

This show grew out of a blog I wrote after I came out of hospital in April 2010, based on notes I took while 'inside'. Writing it was hugely cathartic, especially when it was appreciated by so many friends and fine fellow writers. It can still be read at www.utterspokenword.com/news/?p=408

One of the advantages of a near-fatal illness is the ego-boost you get from hearing so many people are genuinely upset you've almost carked it, and certainly, writing a blog was a much quicker way of explaining what had happened than telling everyone individually – especially when I was still so ill and out of breath. The poems you're about to read as part of the narrative soon followed.

Despite much encouragement, however, attempts to get the blog published came to nothing. So it was a good thing I eventually improved enough – heart failure isn't something I'd say you 'get better' from – to start performing poems about my experience. Eventually I realised I could turn the whole thing into a show. Best take it easy and do it properly, mind – which was why I went to an Apples and Snakes workshop, where

'Heart-stopper' caught the attention of Anthony Shrubsall, Director of Zena Edwards' *Security*.

Even when everything in a show actually happened to you, it still takes *ages* to write it – or rather, to *un*write it, deciding which bits to cut down or leave out, bits which may seem very important to you personally, but don't serve the show. So I'd like to thank Anthony especially, but also everyone who came to read-throughs and previews and helped me shape the show over its two years' development, Lee for tech support, and everyone who's given me advice, reviews, the BHF, CMA, Wellcome Trust and all others who provided press, support (and money, don't forget the money).

I'd also like to thank Apples and Snakes and all the other promoters and audiences who let me try out bits, and the Department of Work and Pensions who provided a writing bursary which enabled me to work on not just the show, but also on returning to a state of health from which I could deliver it. I'd like to thank family and friends for keeping me distracted from death, but most of all, I'd like to thank everyone in the NHS and medical science profession who helped save my life from the echocardiographers, Boston Scientific and Dr Shiu to the woman who has forever won an affectionate place in my memories as 'bum-wipe nurse'. When I give them a copy of this book, I'm sure she'll be thrilled.

The last section of the book comprises material written during, or concerning, the run-up to my illness, convalescence and present time, in chronological thematic order. *Pain don't hurt* was edited from the show due to time constraints, and *All Your Ex-Girlfriends as Soviet Statue Park* due to similarity in pitch with *Beating the Bounds*. The short story *The Day Everybody in the World's Arsehole Disappeared* predates my illness but seems strangely fitting given its medical terminology and theme of the sudden shifting of biological parameters. *Footprints in the Sand* charts my shock religious conversion due to my near-near death experience; from atheist to agnostic. Some will note particular recurring images in these poems; let me just say that for me, Bernini and Ferrero Rocher exemplify the Baroque.

Illustrations throughout are from the show's animations by patternfightperformance.com (Sarah Ruff and Ed Currie). Thanks to them for their patience with my strange demands, imagination and diligent work. Photos are by various people, some of them me.

If you've been affected by any of the issues raised during the show/book/book of the show, or want more information on your heart in general, and we've all got one - well, some people, like me, now have two but it's not really something they're generally very gruntled about - then get hold of some leaflets from the British Heart Foundation – bhf.org.uk. Or for more specific info on any of the cardiomyopathies, the accurately-named and very helpful Cardiomyopathy association, cardiomyopathy.org.

Massive thanks to my Crowdfunder supporters, those with the most dilated, magnanimious tickers first;

Love hearts: James McKay, Douglas Cairns (Sid Ozalid), Young Dawkins, Rob Gullinson, Neil Hume, Daisy Solomons, Mike West (@camdenlight), Richie Brown (@whiffytidings).

Warm hearts: Sophia Blackwell (@sophiablackwell), Jack Jenkins, Lyndsay Jones, Fay Roberts (@fayroberts), Oneiros, Rob Sears, Greg Shreeve.

Big Hearts: Chris Smith, Matthew Bloch (@matthewbloch), Nicky Reeve, Simon Barraclough (@essbarraclough), Dave Bryant (@23Daves), Vicky Cirillo & Mark Underhill, Michael Clift, Joe Evans, A.F. Harrold (@afharrold), Carrie, Gloria and Tyrone Jones, Duncan Law, Gareth Lewis, Thea Martin, Josh Neicho, Tom Phillips (@flashboy), Dave Pickering (@goosefat101), George Pope, Lou Psyche, Rob Richards, Leora Ronel, Simon Ross, Dan Simpson (@dansimpsonpoet), Linda Slawinska, Tom Slawinski, Niall Spooner-Harvey, Jon Ward (@jnthn_xiv), Albert Wassall, Jon Wills.

Sweethearts: Mel Jones, Jacob Sam La Rose (@jsamlarose), Nina McDonagh, Victoria Mitchinson, Kevin Reinhardt, James

Ross (@fkio1), Liz Seacombe, The Tea Poet, Taranga (Andreas), Richard Wright.

Heartbeats: Francis Crot, Kaye Freeman, Lucie Holliday, Rhiannon Hughes, Clare Pollard, Adi Stuart.

May you never have a heart as big as mine was. At least not literally.

RTJ 17.05.2011 – 31.07.12

Denial

Introduction

Hello, I'm Richard Tyrone Jones. I'm ginger, I'm a poet, and I have chronic heart failure.

I'm joking of course. I'm not really ginger. I wish I was joking about the heart failure though – well, no I don't, because that would mean I was joking about having a disease which kills around 24,100 people per year. That would be sick – as sick as I was when I was hospitalised with it in March 2010.

So this is the true story of me, my big heart and how it tried to kill me. It'll be exciting! But not too exciting, because if my heartbeat goes over 188 beats per minute[1] my implantable cardioverter defibrillator will go off, and if my implantable cardioverter de*FIB*rillator goes off... we'll all get catapulted back in time.

But first I should ask the question: Who am I? Or, better, answer the question – who was I? Well, I was a smart, healthy, everywhere-cycling, *['mount' bike, mime cycling]* gym-going, hill-walking, mostly non-alcoholic, *[wave]* non-smoking, Cambridge graduate *['dismount' bike]*. Quite the man about town, I liked to think. I'd fled my dreary West Midlands homeland some years earlier to pursue a glittering career in London as a poet, traversing its green spaces to gain inspiration, following in the footsteps of Betjeman, Keats and

---

[1] Actually 250bpm at the time of writing, but I wanted to get a *Back to the Future* reference into the show.

Plath. Well maybe not *so much* Plath. Not the *best* career role model...

But all that was thrown into jeopardy when I managed to somehow get mystery heart failure that would leave my distended, saggy, water bomb-balloon organ pumping out just 10-15% of its capacity – and I'm still talking about my heart here - when a healthy heart pumps out about 60%. How did that happen to *me*? I mean, I assumed that heart failure only happened to genuinely old people, like forty or fifty year-olds.

How did I manage to not notice for quite a long time that the most vital organ of my body was rebelling against me? And was my doom in any way connected to the fact that, less than a month earlier, to mark my thirtieth birthday, I had held my own mock funeral, with me lying in a real coffin throughout, flanked by women in black holding fatherless ginger children, with hymns, tributes from friends, the reading of the will, and professionally-printed programmes?

Well, probably. But it was a lot of fun.

As you can probably tell from that, I was quite a morbid person anyway; in fact I used to often suffer from serious depression. So since being so ill, have I become more hopeful, more thankful for life? Or am I even more of a miserable git now I've really got something to moan about? And how about the other 63,499[2] people per year who contract, or die from, heart failure, but aren't me?

Do they matter?

Well, let's start at what probably wasn't the beginning...

---

[2] From incidence rates in the Hillingdon Heart Failure Study we estimate that there are just around 63,500 new cases of heart failure each year in the UK. Applying a 62% one-year survival rate to this figure means that just over 24,100 of those diagnosed from heart failure die within a calendar year. (www.bhf.org.uk)

The run-down run-up

A short while before I actually *felt* ill, my louche, aristocratic GP, who listened to classical music during consultations, had diagnosed me with atrial fibrillation – a 'regularly irregular', or 'bebop' heart beat. He merely advised me to 'cut down on the caffeine, and take aspirin regularly' – which I duly did. So when, towards the end of 2009, I began to feel apathy, lethargy and even not wanting to drink or go out womanising (very much) – for a poet that's antithetical behaviour – I put it down to my cyclical depression – for a poet that's very much thetical behaviour – then booked myself some cognitive-behavioural therapy, and a holiday to Rome in December to visit Keats' grave (you know, cheer myself up a bit!) I then ploughed on with my normal punishing schedule. Of getting up at eleven, writing half a limerick, then spending the rest of the day replenishing my bank of unsuitable metaphors by watching 1980s sci-fi films.

But further symptoms began to show themselves: not only fainting fits worthy of an Edwardian damsel (and I really wasn't wearing my corset *that* tight), but coruscating migraines which I'd last experienced about ten years ago at the end of university – though they'd previously disappeared when I had both all my wisdom teeth and all academic ambition simultaneously removed. So I redoubled my efforts to get fit, cycling everywhere *['mount' bike, pedal furiously]* to combat Boris Johnson's fare hikes, and my own ill-health *['dismount' bike],* doing press-ups and sit-ups (almost) every day, and even joining Archway gym. I was dedicated. *[2-3 lunges].*

But, like a cartoon Jamaican swimming in Egypt's longest river, I... was in denial. *[Pause for groans, tomatoes, &c.]*[3] The more exercise I did, the worse I felt, till in March 2010, one month after my funeral, I was on the jogging machine jogging, listening to deathstep drum & bass[4] and watching Countdown.

---

[3] Oh come on, I almost died! I think I'm allowed one godawful dad joke per show.

[4] This style of music is best described as the sound of a medieval knight getting a wasp trapped in his suit of armour then falling down eight storeys of fire escape into a metal skip.

For the first time ever, I got the target number bang on, and it must've been the effort of doing all three things at once that invoked a migraine so huge the Met Office could have named it. It drove me home from the gym indefinitely, followed by two aftershocks, one day after the other.

I came down with a horrible mutating cold-cum-sore throat-cum-hacking cough-cum-nose-faucet through which I bravely, yet stupidly, yet professionally, kept on gigging, despite by then being unable to cycle, walking very slowly and breathlessly like the Stay-Puft Marshmallow Man, suffering occasional chest pains like I had myself been hit in my side by a proton accelerator. I told myself I just had a chest infection or a stitch!

See, the problem was that I *thought* the problem was with my brain, or my lungs, because those were where the symptoms were. My GP even sent me for an MRI[5] brain scan. This was like being shut in a drawer for twenty minutes being forced to listen to avant-garde Finnish techno – so not too different to my normal leisure pursuits! The scan was negative, so next, they booked me in to wear a twenty-four hour electrocardiogram monitor, which also goes by the far sexier name of 'Holter strap' *[Projection of sensors onto the body]*. Then, an echocardiogram where they look at your heart using a... radar thingy.

---

[5] Magnetic resonance imaging.

The night before the echocardiogram, I was awake, hacking my lungs up, all night and shuffled, sleepless, to the emergency GPs in the morning, who listened to my chest and prescribed antibiotics. I tweeted 'Hooray! I have a mere chest infection, and not the incipient heart disease I was petrified I had.'

THAT will teach me. Later that day, the 'echo' – and this was the first time I'd ever seen inside my own body - turned out to be intimate, somewhat homoerotic, somehow religious, and definitely reminiscent of the 1986 Dennis Quaid film 'Inner Space'...

sorted.
23 Apr 10

rtjpoet rtyronejones
back from hospital AGAIN. I hereby unconditionally repent of my previous mockery of death and apologise to any offended deities.
22 Apr 10

rtjpoet rtyronejones
Thanks for all the lovely messages. I'm now out of hospital, pacemakered up and off to recuperate in Wolverhampton, my ancestral seat x
17 Apr 10

rtjpoet rtyronejones
Feeling better but still in hospital. Not sure when out. Thanks for all the lovely messages, cards and visits.
8 Apr 10

rtjpoet rtyronejones
Hooray! I have a mere chest infection, and not the incipient heart disease I was petrified I had. Still, off to my echocardiogram....
30 Mar 10

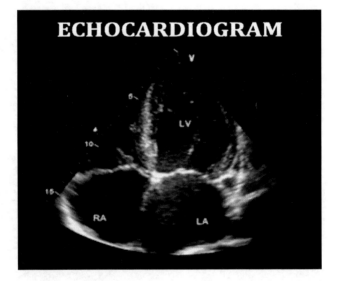

Echo

Strong black
hands in
thin white
gloves
grease
my chest
& apply
the probe.

Like gazing down into a
modernist cathedral, from the atrial vault
we see the flapping   tapestries of the mitral valves;
like spastic butterflies,   or the clapping of white Baptists
who can't quite dance in   time. We descend, to the floor of
this bloody transept, our viewscreen that of a bathysphere trip,
nine fathoms deep into your own corpus. Track left, enhance,
I imagine: Dante in a sub battling an exo-suited henchman.
The soundtrack – bllrrrruush, bllrrrruush – a wobbleboard,
digitised; a clashing red blood cell tide. Was that a cross
on the wall? An elder priest walks in, white haired,
advises 'take a look at that again.' It's not a cross,
more like a puckered anus blowing us a kiss. A
roadblock. Crater. A heart attack in training,
a stroke, gestating. In my mind's ear, I hear
the guy whisper '*bluuuuudclaaaaat*'.
It's a grainy picture, but it's black
and white. I won't be going
to that party tonight.

The echocardiographer didn't *really* whisper 'bludclaaat', that would've been tremendously insensitive. And racially stereotypical.[6]

But after the echo, I did see a rather *effete* doctor, who seemed to enjoy comfortingly patting my leg a bit too much. Maybe that was an attempt to distract from the fact he was telling me that, yes, I had a blood clot in my heart which could break off causing a stroke or cardiac arrest elsewhere in my bloodstream, and that I'd have to be admitted. I thought this was the most terrible health news I'd receive for a very long time. THAT will teach me.

For he then explained that my heart had also become dilated - stretched - by two centimetres, when a heart's normally only the size of a fist - the fist at my centre had unclenched. And they had no idea what had caused this. You'll remember, I'd thought I had just a chest infection. Well, turns out I had a chest infection *as well.*

So at least I was right about one thing!

---

[6] It won't surprise you to learn, though, that the echocardiographer was the coolest man in the hospital. After all, he was the ultra sound guy...

Admission

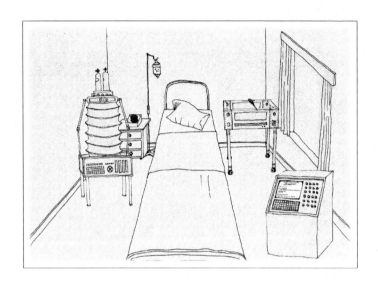

Admission

And so into hospital, very unwell,
coughing my lungs up with heart failure phleghm,
put on four different drugs, put to bed,
docs in at all hours to suck up my blood,
I was hooked up to drips and to blood pressure sleeves,
a number of numbers slowly dropping on a screen
pulse monitors stuck to my self-harming chest -
still, I had a nice view and a room to myself...

Given a load of blood had just clotted inside my heart, and also given my atrial fibrillation, every doctor I spoke to seemed amazed I hadn't already been put on the anticoagulant Warfarin™, which is also used as a rat poison and... I *think* I've got their first album. Roargh! *[Optional 'Horns' hand-gesture.]*

I was subjected to innumerable identical interrogations which I always answered thus:

- No, I'm not really a *bad* alcoholic. I've always liked to think I was rather a *good* one.

- No, I don't really party that hard. I have sampled a *pinch* of mephedrone but only enough to annoy the Daily Mail.

- No, none of my family have died early of heart problems – we much prefer to go slowly mental instead.

- Italy in December, but Italy's hardly *foreign* is it?

- No, I've not been in close contact with any ruminant mammals, what are you insinuating?

Seriously, I was very curious to find out what exactly had been the 'trigger event' for my heart failure – had I just been incredibly unlucky, with a virus spreading from chest to heart, or was there some hidden cause?

Either way, if you get heart failure, in addition to Warfarin, they'll put you on beta-blockers to slow the heart rate, stop it damaging itself, and ACE inhibitors to hopefully shrink it and return some of its elasticity. In addition, I was given extra anti-coagulant injections in my belly, which left me as black and blue as if nurses had been coming in in the night and pummeling me in the stomach.

But this pharmacopeia worked *too* well, lowering my already-low blood pressure still further so that, five days into my stay, I was hit by a force 10 coughing attack which blew me off course to the cardiac care unit. Pale of face, full of phleghm, and drained of energy, I still had the presence of mind, as I was carted off, to issue a feeble royal wave. This reassured my sister who'd come down to visit from my ancestral seat – of Dudley[7-]

---

[7] If I want to make someone laugh I say I'm from Dudley. If I want to impress someone I say Wolverhampton, given its city status. The reality is, I am from Sedgley, which is in between.

but I didn't reassure myself at all. I began to realise there was a genuinely large chance I was going to die. I made my will.

For real this time.

Horrible bit

Oh, so many fond hospital memories to share with you! That night, the doctors decided it would be a good idea to feed a 'line' directly into my heart – a tube with which they could measure its pressure and feed drugs directly in. It was too dangerous, given my fragile condition, to give me general anaesthetic for this 'procedure' – they don't like to call them 'operations' these days – so I was sedated and given local anaesthetic. Despite this, I still had to choke back my bubbly phleghm all the way through and could still *feel* the surgeons cutting my neck and failing to get the line in the right way for the first couple of attempts.

Another Horrible bit

Now, here's a tip. If any of you think being so weak and bed-bound that you have to lever yourself up to - ahem - pass a motion into what is basically a papier-mache hat, then have your bottom wiped clean by a nurse - no matter how buxom - might in any way prove an erotic experience, you are wrong. Especially when the nurse in question doesn't actually do that *thorough* a job of cleansing your anal cleft of the by now frankly orange, wet cement-like ...ackymoomoo, and you have to actually get rid of her with an excuse -*'I need a wee'* - so you can finish feebly wiping it properly yourself without hurting her feelings.

And here's another tip. Saying to that nurse, as she attends to your posterior, 'Some blokes would probably get off on something like this, *but not me, I can assure you'* is, on balance, unlikely to assure her.

Day after day of palpitations, nausea and weakness, rudely awoken at all hours for blood tests and awful food, *[get up and hobble to look out of imaginary window]* gazing out at Hampstead Heath in the Springtime, wondering if I'd ever be able to walk its slopes again. I knew I could leave at any time. If I simply ran out of there as fast as I could, *[slightly raise balls of feet]* I could leave in a way that would mean I'd never have to have another blood test, see another doctor - do anything - again. And it was tempting, because that way, at least I'd *get* to run, feel fresh air on my face, once more. A sample line from my diary at this time: 'You want Disneyland, you get Dignitas.'

[Collapse tired on the bed again].

Tired Jokes

Physically, you don't 'fight' illness,
There's no bravery for the bedridden.
it's not strength you need, it's patience.
you just sit there, take your medicine.
Without energy even to fear,
leached out through toilet, through lungs, by sedation,
wanting to, fearing to, straining to feel
but suffering, ironically, tear constipation,
then family and friends bring you more than mere gifts
they give heart, when you've none left in reserve
by showing how, if you 'went', they'd be bereft.
So I make us laugh at that tired joke, death,
to pass on my love, hide my concern,
but mostly, 'cos that's my behavioural script.

Pipes & drainage

The next day I found out the hospital in fact had wheelchair-toilets – commodes, they're called! So yes, you could sit down to 'go'. A few tears escaped then.

And it was only at this point, by the way, that the doctors put me back *on* the antibiotics they'd taken me *off* on entry to the hospital (in case they interfered with the Warfarin). I recognised an almost instant improvement as one variety of phleghm (brown, left lung, texture of Wrigley's chewing gum) caused by the infection, now lifted, leaving me with just the other variety (white, both lungs, how to describe its frothy richness... every time I hawked it up it made me quite fancy a McDonald's milkshake Nom nom nom nom nom, I'm loving it...) This phleghm was caused by the water in blood that was not being pumped out of my heart instead being forced through capillaries into the lungs.

So on 6th April, one week into my stay, it was time for my angiogram, which is where someone called Angie comes in dressed as a chicken and sings you a song. No it isn't. It's a delightful procedure where they open up your groin and spray up slightly radioactive chemicals to find out if your arteries are furred up like a sixty-year old alcoholic butcher's. So in came a cute nurse (not bum-wipe nurse) who I would have fancied, had I not been rendered *almost* completely impotent, in a situation in which *complete* impotence would certainly be preferable. She told me that before the procedure, half my *mons pubis* and the top of my thigh would have to be shaved. I thought *'hell-o',* in the voice of Leslie Phillips, but sadly the only help she could offer was two cheap safety razors and a sachet of liquid soap.

Yet, only once almost flooding the ward by blocking the shower with my shorn-off ginger pubes, I eventually managed the task, and modeling the traditional fetching hospital paper pants, I then had to go hungry all day before they eventually did the much-delayed angiogram... through my wrist. *[Close legs]*. Traditional hospital wind-up, perhaps!

And, as it 'would not have affected the way they treated me' they didn't do the biopsy they'd promised - scraping a sliver of meat from the inside of my heart - to find out what the 'trigger event' was. So we'll never discover which is more perilous: going to Rome, contact with ruminant mammals, or sniffing the now-banned industrial plant food stimulant mephedrone.

A bag of kittens

What I did discover was my arterial plumbing was thankfully not blocked. So I had heart *failure*, yes, but no heart *disease*. Next night, I felt good enough to get out of bed for the first time in two days, and, with permission, unhooked myself from my drip, checked nothing was coming out of that 'line' in my neck, and toileted in the night without collapsing. Propped-up again in the adjustable bed so I didn't choke on my phleghm in the night, I returned to sleep. And a short while later woke up in a small pond of my own blood collected in the bed's angle. Not enough to drown a bag of kittens in, but enough to bathe a small chihuahua. It was, on balance, a good thing I'd happened to wake up when I did.

When they removed this line the next day, one doctor told me that not only had it been completely useless, and an MRSA risk, but that I'd also had a crust of dried blood round my neck where they'd put it in for several days, though no-one had told me. It was like a... black pudding necklace. If I'd known it was there I would... I would have been picking it off and eating it as a snack. I'm from the West Midlands, I *love* black pudding, me!

Diagnosis

The heart failure nurse

After eleven days, on 9th April, I finally got my official diagnosis – 'Idiopathic Dilated Cardiomyopathy.' Translation: Mystery big strained baggy inelastic heart muscles of an old man. So I won a visit from 'The Heart Failure Nurse'. I told her that, with a title like that, she'll never prove as popular a bedside visitor as The Tooth Fairy, say; might need rebranding. She told me that, 'with a heart like that, you're now more at risk of developing cardiac rhythms *not conducive to life*; might need an implantable cardioverter defibrillator.'[8] So she won that exchange of wits.

That was the good news. Less good news was that she also couldn't promise me that the drugs I was on would actually bring about recovery. I couldn't really pay attention to what she was saying to me after that.... *'Bla bla blah possible heart transplant bla bla blah...'*

---

[8] Acts as a pacemaker, but also as an internal automatic defibrillator in case your heart stops.

Yet despite all this, I had been beginning to feel *slightly* better, and my reward for feeling better was to be transferred! ...to the mummy room at the British Museum. Well, that's what the collective ward seemed like, being so full of truly old, cadaverous geezers. But worse, the next morning, they made the mistake of sending in a quite incongruously foxy Italian-American student doctor to take my case history. What happened? Well, the title of this next poem is...

Heart-stopper

The ward's tourniquets sport smiling cartoon Draculas;
All night, old men's alarms have burst my dreams.
A med. student, red-nailed, raven-haired, immaculate,
asks so many questions it's like she wants to date me.
She reads my wrist with slow, sharp-clawed precision
then joins the rounds. If I were well, I'd like to rip her skirt off.
And at that thought, dark lightning tears my chest -
sweat-drenched, I paw for oxygen, panic button,
it's like my plug's been pulled – breath fades so fast
I whimper 'Mum, I love you' with my last....
But the heart monitor nurse bursts in, whips back the curtain,
shouts out 'He's had a gap!' The rest
dash back, ask the student: 'can you get his shirt off?'
She panics 'How?' They just cut it, like on television.
I'm flailing, failing, they're about to defibrillate me
– 'Clear' - But two have already stabbed in canulas;
adrenalin stakes slow paths through my bloodstream.
I'm alive, but empty, trembling. 'Vaso-vascular'.

Luckily for me, that episode meant I got my own room again to recover in, shaking like a hostage. Unluckily for my own self-mythologising, however, it turned out my heart hadn't actually stopped, just slowed down immensely – with a long 'gap' between beats. I can't decide if that means I *can* boast that I almost died, or merely that I *almost* almost died. But I tell you, four seconds *[four second pause]* seems a very long time without a heartbeat.

Ironically, the shirt I was wearing that got cut up was this very one, by similarly-morbid conceptual artist Charlotte Young. At the time I couldn't decide what words of wit I was going to put in the gaps. Luckily, my near-near death experience solved that problem, and it's now a kind of poem itself: 'My HEART (ALMOST) died of DILATED CARDIOMYOPATHY and all I got was this lousy t-shirt CUT UP BY THE CRASH TEAM'. [9]

Oh, and who was the heartbeat monitor nurse who noticed my 'gap' and saved my life? The very same nurse who had been so poo at wiping poo. But which is the more important life skill, really... in the end?

---

[9] When I was nine, watching cheesy hospital drama 'Casualty' and they cut someone's shirt open in the operating theatre, I always thought 'oh, what a terrible waste of clothes.' A thought almost immediately replaced, in 50% of cases, by 'ooh, some boobies!'

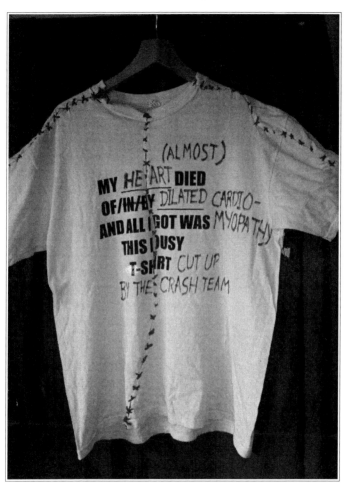

(T-shirts now available in the foyer.)

More animated characters

I'm also sorry it's been mostly about me so far. Lots of other people were in hospital, with lots of different heart problems. Some of them even younger and fitter than me. I should have asked them what they'd got – if only the British Heart Foundation did an i-spy book of congenital heart defects and cardiomyopathies for those in hospital, it'd be a great way to go round ticking them off, to make friends *and* raise awareness!

But I wasn't yet thinking about what would make a good one-person show, more about what would make a good inscription for my memorial bench. (Richard Tyrone Jones, 1980 – 2010, he was a bastard, tramps get priority, I'd decided).

One fellow patient I did get the full story on - by eavesdropping on his mobile conversation - was a twenty year old guy. When I tell you I gave him the affectionate nickname 'Coke man', perhaps you can guess what had caused his heart attack.

Corrected transposition

'Yeah, I've 'ad 'art attack, bruv. Too much charlie!
Was laid in bed *two daze* till I flipped,
went *stir crazy*, bruv, rrripped out me drips
bust aht dem doors like a one-man army!
Why? Cos, brer, I need-ed-a-cig-a-rette!
Nah I collapsed, straight back in intensive care.
Oh but when they done that echo fing yeah,
they found like I got dis 'cardiac defect'?
Yeah, me arteries are swapped the wrong way round!
Noone's never noticed all fru m'life.
Don't do no harm, but it's funny to fink.
Nah, I'm leaving tomorrow, gotta get *out* -
too much like prison 'ere, d'you get me bruv?!
Listen when I'm back d'you, er.... *need* anyfink'?'

I wonder if Coke man suspected his conversation would be turned into a Petrarchan sonnet? He made me feel like a very responsible patient. Now I hid my phone and wallet in my pillow while I slept, just in case, but next day it turned out he was quite friendly - in fact he left me his smoothie and a telly card. Which just goes to show: you should never judge a drug dealer by their telephone manner.

Later, I found myself opposite the opposite of Coke man – an incredibly fit black guy in his late 30s who maintained 'I feel fine! Never felt better!' but whose blood pressure was actually over twice mine (mine was around 70, his around 170[10]). 'They've been trying to get that down three days! They keep asking me if I've been on drugs! I've never even touched drugs! I've never needed *them* to approach the laydees, you know what I mean? Some of my friends, they need to get off their face to talk to the laydees, but I never have done, I've always had plenty of laydees interested in me!' Only one *laydee* came and visited him though.

---

[10] Both figures are systolic (maximum) blood pressure, ie 'on' the pulse rather than 'off' it. Desirable blood pressure is 90-119mmHg. I had the opposite of hypertension, the confusingly-named hypotension. 'mmHg' or 'millimetre of mercury', the unit of measurement of blood pressure, is the pressure exerted at the base of a column of fluid exactly 1 mm high, when the density of the fluid is exactly 13.5951 g/cm^3, at a place where the acceleration of gravity is exactly 9.80665 m/s^2. So that's cleared that up.

Demographics

What he had was hypertension. As my fellow poet Tim Wells, who has it, complains: 'the fing that's probably going to kill you sounds like a '70s disco band'. What I had was the opposite – hypotension, low blood pressure, caused by my failing, stretched cardiac muscle.

I had absolutely no idea so many different things could go wrong with the human heart. But I don't want you thinking that heart problems affect mostly men, that's a common misconception. I just wasn't on a mixed ward. In fact, heart and circulatory disease kill one in three men *and* one in three women. That's three times as many as breast cancer – not that I'm trying to play 'fatal disease top trumps' here.

While we're talking demographics, what concerned me more was, well, to what extent was this dilated cardiomyopathy genetic? Had I passed my condition to my offspring? Oh, yeah, my offspring – sorry, did I forget to mention them? Well, there's a reason for that - I've never met them. Not because I 'doinged' their 'babymammas' then ran off but because, well, I cheated. Before I knew about all this, I was a sperm donor. Turns out, Cambridge graduate semen is quite highly prized – even if you are ginger. In fact, while I'm coming clean - this is how ginger people breed. After all, no-one's actually ever seen any of us mate successfully, in the wild, have they? So they're just my... 'biokids'. All... twelve of them.[11]

---

[11] This may explain the number of dad jokes in the show.

There's literally a whole other show to be written about the speculative emotional kaleidoscope in my head about them, but as soon as I could stumble to a quiet spot on the ward, I phoned the clinic to let them know what had happened to me, because I do have a big heart, both literally and figuratively. The clinic and I both agreed it'd be best if my sperm stayed in the fridge until I got the results of my genetic tests, which... shall be revealed.

Operation

But more personally, it was time for another procedure. I was, as usual, concerned I might die during it and so spent my possible last hours relaxing by indulging my two favourite pastimes - listening to deathstep drum & bass and reading a H.P. Lovecraft story, 'The Rats in the Walls'. *[reading]* "The walls... were *filled with rats*."

But this small risk was necessary, because the implantable cardioverter defibrillator I was about to have fitted would correct both any too-slow heartbeats (bradycardia) and too-fast heartbeats (tachycardia) – as well as shocking me back to life if my heart ever stopped.

In theatre, I requested they change the radio to classical music, arguing successfully that 'If I do die on the table, I'm not going to die listening to Phil fucking Collins.' But in actual fact, the operation was brilliant! Again, I had to remain conscious throughout. Yet this time, the sedatives worked so fantastically that by near the end I was quietly pleading for more, like a Dickensian whelp. The surgeon was very efficient (Dr Shiu, I'd recommend him – he's Chinese, not a shoe with a face who does operations, I wasn't that out of it). He popped the debrillator in under my collar bone with all the assurance of an experienced kebab-shop owner easing a falafel into a pitta that seems too small for it to fit and, just as he expertly stitched me closed, Wagner's Ride of the Valkyries swooped onto the radio. Off my face on Diazepam, that counted as a moment.

Two days later I *felt* ready to go home, even managing to sell a copy of my book (Germline, Vintage Poison Press, RRP £6.99) to a nice Greek businessman called George. To be fair, he had just had a heart attack, he couldn't escape my sales pitch. I gave another to that cute nurse I'd been chatting up. I thought it best not to get out of practice. So, I finally hobbled out into the Spring sunshine... to get home and relax in my own garden with a nice cup of (decaf) tea...

...And another two days later, I was back in hospital again after almost-collapsing at the anti-coagulant clinic. And this time, it was worse – because it was in my hometown, Dudley. If anyone's been to Dudley, you won't be surprised to hear that the nurses there are not as attractive as in London, partly because they all sound like this:

'Will yow stop callin' moy Scraggle?'[12]

But while I was there, for three days, they did sort out one of my problems, for...

---

[12] Comic Sans is the publishing industry's standard font to indicate a West Midlands accent.

Gratuitous limerick

A relatively young and dashing heart failure patient from Dudley
had phleghm that was thick, white and bubbly
till a diuretic prescription[13]
made his water retention
gush out in a notably good wee.

It lasted four minutes, filled two papier-mache bottles and the next day, I weighed two pounds lighter. It was the best piss of my life![14]

---

[13] Furosemide 40mg, since you ask.

[14] Even better than the one I had after I accidentally trapped myself in a porch for seven hours.

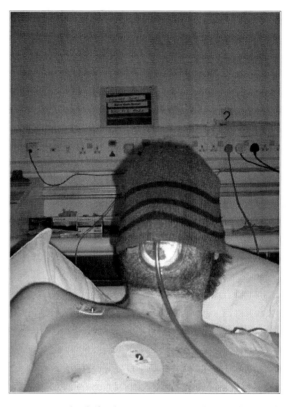

Sometimes it can be difficult trying to get to sleep in hospital, what with the nurses leaving all the bloody lights on.

Prognosis

A convoluted convalescence

So, I was finally out. But still frail, faint and frightened. Plus, in so much pain, even showering left me gasping for fifteen minutes, with so little improvement that I feared I was going to have to: be on benefits for the rest of my life, get a mobility scooter, and, on the *negative* side, move permanently back in with my parents in Dudley. I was determined this wouldn't happen. Here's the poem I wrote while desperately trying to hang onto my London residence, and lifestyle, despite realising that I was, for the foreseeable future... *disabled.*

Beating the bounds

This Summer, my friends have been collecting wrist-bands from festivals.
I've been doing the same but with the name-tags from hospitals.

They say, 'the first step is the hardest'; that's not true.
It's almost as if I'm still normal, for the first few,
but my first rest must come after forty paces, then at twenty,

ten, five – I'm the frog in Zeno's second paradox,
will he ever reach his pond? Or just gaze down at wasted legs
which, this time last month, were still thick as a toad's.

If the vessels in my defective bloodstream were stretched, they'd
                                           reach
the length of whole borders, jump hill, vale and watercourse,
once did. I used to roam as far afield as Luton, Leeds, Milton Keynes,

for a schools gig. Now, Eastward, I can inch to the chip shop, but they
                                          get cold
before they get home. Westbound, Archway is my border, but I then
must bus back, as now each return journey is an uphill struggle.

Like me, my eighty-eight year old Gramps takes Warfarin.
3mg to my six. Diuretics: he's 20mg, me, eighty. I've borrowed his stick.
But I'm also on ACE inhibitors, beta blockers, co-codamol to firm up
                                          my squits,

and Diazepam to stop me waking in the night choking on my own
throat,
spasming on misfiring neurons which maybe, once, were hopes.
I stagger my trips, based on benches and low walls. On rainy days

I stay in to save crushing whole families of snails. Leaning
against lampposts to let pushchairs push past, heavily breathing,
I'll soon get a reputation as the local creepy man.

My heart strains to escape, or keep up - a trapped pigeon, a crap clock.
Its device would resurrect me faster than Christ, but rather
than install a new lease of life, I feel I'm in my 30-day reprieve.

I'm an invalidated warranty. They say home is where the heart is, but
home is only where the heart will let you roam, and my security
barriers
are the tidal currents of water retention, keeping me docked,

stinging me in the kidneys if I stumble into them, my internal tasers.
I used to walk as far as I wished. Now I don't even wish to walk.
I fear the day will come when I'll stop running even in my dreams.

Keeping it together

I now had to say goodbye to walking holidays, to foreign travel, even sex. I mean, it still *just about* worked, but in my state I was no longer a catch, was I? Sexual relationships were something which had once loomed over every aspect of my life, but were now of merely historical significance... to the extent that I wrote a poem called 'All your ex-girlfriends as Soviet statue park'.[15]

I was still hacking up so much phlegm, I felt I may as well look up the correct technical term for it: 'therapeutic aspiration', which sounds like a sort of hippy neuro-linguistic programming technique.

Despite all this, I largely kept it together. Psychologically, I mean. Not my phlegm. This was strange, because previously, under stressful situations like exams or breakups, I have gone *completely* to pieces. Perhaps it was because this was something physical I *had* to face up to. Or perhaps I finally realised, as the self-help books I was reading all parrot, 'you can't always choose your personal situation, but you *can* choose your personal response to it.' So in my diary, I resolved to consider the possible advantages ...of having heart failure. 'Therapeutic aspiration,' if you will.

---

[15] See 'Complications'.

Reasons to be cheerful (about heart failure)

1. In the middle of a recession, I've enjoyed a raise. (I say a raise, I switched from Working Tax Credit to Incapacity Benefit, that's... similar.)

2. I used to get depressed about my lack of achievement compared to my peers – I was at University with people like Tim Key and Mark Watson – but now I've got a brilliant excuse! I've not got a girlfriend – I've got heart failure! Or a job – I've got heart failure! I don't even have a theme for my first solo show – I've got heart failure! - no, wait a second...

3. I don't get stressed any more, because I'm on so many drugs to lower my heart rate that it's actually a physical impossibility for me to get stressed. Or excited. Or feel any of those pesky canards we call emotion.

4. No drinking or womanising will save me thousands of pounds!

5. My ICD (tap it) will, if I have a cardiac arrest, reboot me time and again, potentially for hours until the battery runs out – so essentially, I'm immortal. The only way to kill me is to cut off my head. Technically, I'm a Highlander. (I'm ready to say goodbye, *Bumphf!* I'm being drawn down a long, dark, tunnel, yes Jesus, I'm coming towards the light... *Bumphf!* PLEASE. LET. ME. DIE. *Bumphf!*)

6. But most importantly, and most seriously, now that I've stared death in the skull, I realise everything else I've ever been worried about – reviews, money, sex, hamsters, pales into insignificance. People say 'oh, nothing matters if you've got your health.'

Wrong. If you've got your health, you take it for granted, and waste all your time worrying about petty rubbish which, if you've *not* got your health, doesn't mean a thing to you. So next time some girl is crying because she's lost her mobile or mooncup, or a comic throws a hissy fit on stage because an audience doesn't get his jokes, I couldn't care less, you spoilt brats - I've got heart failure, I'm lucky to be alive.

After all that looking on the bright side, I bet you all wish you had heart failure too don't you?

Eplerenone and Digoxin

But a positive mental attitude can't fix breathlessness, pain and limited mobility. It looked like I wouldn't make it to something I'd done so much work for - the August 2010 Edinburgh Fringe. Especially when, in June, I found myself back in hospital - for the fifth time that year - with my heart apparently pumping out just *seven percent* of its capacity. But while in there, doctors dashed two new drugs into my cocktail: Eplerenone, which lessens blood volume sufficiently that the heart pumps less blood but it pumps it more efficiently, and Digoxin, from the foxglove, aka the poison 'digitalis', which augments hemodynamics by increasing calcium ion levels in the 'sarcoplasmic reticulum'. [16] No, I don't really have a clue *how* it works either.

But... it did. I didn't want to give myself false hope, but I couldn't deny that yes, soon I could actually walk, only stopping to stop gasp against a wall every 10, 20, then 40 yards. Not overdoing it, Edinburgh became possible - in fact, walking very slowly, by the end of the month I'd made it to the top of Calton Hill. That sounds like it took me a whole month to walk up a hill – no, it took an hour. But I'd improved so much just to manage even that.[17] In fact, I felt like one of the old people in *Cocoon (1985).*

---

[16] *I'm sure I've got their second album...*

[17] *Oh, and we got a four-star review too – 'prepare to be left speechless by the tongues of these capable bards' (ThreeWeeks). Didn't bring anyone in, mind.*

What becomes of the broken-hearted?

A Spot of Eugenics

But most importantly, we come those results of *my* genetic test – and therefore, potentially, of my biokiddies. Here comes the science part! So, within *dilated* cardiomyopathy alone, there are at least 40 known genes that give rise to 40+ different variants of the disease: from those that mean a fifty year old has to take some tablets and it easy, to the nasty lamin A/C gene, which can kill young people without warning. My test for that one was... and remember, this matters because these kids are the future of the ginger race here... *negative,* so they won't have it either. Phew!

As for the other 39+ genes – well, I'm actually not waiting for *the results of* a genetic test. Like every other cardiomyopathy sufferer I'm waiting for *the genetic tests themselves* to become cheap enough that the NHS can do them. But genetics, stem cell research, the growing of new hearts in tanks, all takes time, money, patience: essentially, a properly-funded, non-privatised, NHS.

In the meantime, should I be allowed to have children myself? I say 'myself' - with a woman I mean. One I've actually met. What about people who might carry genes for... cancer? Deafness? Short-sightedness? Hare lip? Not being able to rrrroll your r's? 23,000 protein-coding genes must be copied to make each human;[18] enough to ensure all of us *will* have faults

---

[18] Stein, L. D. 2004. "Human Genome: End of the Beginning," *Nature* 431, 915-916. Available online.

in some of them. So many terms, describing so many conditions we might carry without knowing. Which is why this poem, a rip-off of – sorry, tribute to - Tom Lehrer, is called...

Terms & Conditions

There's cancer and porphyria and hypercalciuria
adrenal hypoplasia, dystrophia myotonica
and hypochondroplasia, 5 Leiden thrombophilia
And hyperoxaluria, methemoglobinemia.
Classic galactosemia and sickle-cell anemia
ataxia, hemophilia and beta-thalassemia,
propionic acidemia, hyperphenylalaninemia, (gasp)
and otospondylomegaepiphyseal dysplasia.

There's Cerebral autosomal dominant arteriopathy
with subcortical infarcts, leukoencephalopathy,
acrocephaly, obesity, and compression neuropathy,
dilated, hypertrophic, and arrhythmogenic right ventricular
cardiomyopathy.
Chondrodystrophy, D-glycerate dehydrogenase deficiency,
and nonclassic type demyelinogenic leukodystrophy,
hypoxanthine-guanine phosphoribosyl transferase deficiency,
*adreno*leukodystrophy, Duchenne muscular dystrophy

and Bourneville phakomatosis, perioral lentiginosis,
Tay-Sachs disease and also type one neurofibromatosis,
craniofacial dysostosis, plain old cystic fibrosis –
dermatosparaxis and mucopolysaccharidosis.
There's cretinism, dwarfism and hyperandrogenism,
pantothenate kinase-associated neurodegeneration,
colour blindness, idiopathic pulmonary hypertension
and fragile X and triple X and XXXXX syndromes.

And those are just the ones that have had write-ups in The Lancet
So if you're expecting perfect kids I don't fancy your chances....

And the moral of the story is...

So, what's the moral of this story? The moral of this story is simple. Don't have heart failure. If you feel heart failure approaching, do try and... nip it in the bud! Chest pains, migraines, frothy phleghm, fainting, exercise intolerance, go to the doctor and don't stop pestering till you've had an ECG.[19] Don't let them fob you off with a BCG, or an EGG – that's just an egg - because each of our DNA signatures seal and conceal our own horrible health fates, and we must face up to them; they don't just affect us, but friends, family, society at large.

I was lucky – for someone who'd been so unlucky. I still can't cycle or run too quickly, but, well, who here gets angry when they get stuck behind old people walking down the street? I was overjoyed when that first happened because it meant 'hurray, I'm faster than an old person again!' My echo in October 2010 revealed my heart capacity was back up to 25%. (That meant I could tackle a 1:4 gradient.) It had shrunk in size by one centimetre. The clot had gone! After the echo I even walked home across Hampstead Heath on an inspiringly beautiful day, six months after I'd gazed out over it wondering if I'd ever do that again. I even came up with a poem. Now I can walk for miles. All those months of painful trudging, and all I needed was... more drugs!

And has it affected my outlook? Yes. I still have to take nine different drugs every day; see doctors every month. Will do till

---

[19] *Electrocardiogram.*

I die. I still feel down. I still have days I'm completely exhausted. But I'm much more thankful for every day I have left, especially the bad ones, because... they remind me just how much I've generally improved.

So could I say that my having heart failure has been a *good* thing?

Well, I still wouldn't *recommend* it, but on a personal development level... yes.

Because...

Now every tenner feels to me
as if it's worth a million
Now every song's a symphony
(except for Robby Williams).
Now every time I'm tired I think
'at least thank god I'm breathing!'
and every time I lose my breath,
at least my heart's still beating.

Thank goodness I can walk,
although I can't walk very fast,
for every step's a giant leap
because it's not my last.
Some folks say 'oh you've been so brave',
but the reason I've not cried
is that now my life has meaning
...because I almost died.

Now even the centre of Luton
seems a quaint historic town
All my clothes are Louis Vuitton –
because they're not medical gowns.
Now every open mic's a gig,
and every gig is Wembley
and every meal's a gourmet one –
now my strawberry tart's less trembly.

See, I thought I would be in pain
for the rest of a shortened life -
But as my health has been regained
every girl's a potential wife (hell-o!)
I've retarmac'ed my libidinous parking space
yes, I've got back my sex drive[20] (groan)
but it's sacred now, to feel profane
...because I almost died.

Now every price tag's ASDA price
every slum's a mansion
each poem I write's a masterpiece
despite its crap ...scansion.
Each B&B's the Marriott
each 'not to be''s a 'be'
Each poet I read's a laureate
and Everyman is me.

Every splinter is a relic
every measure is a bottle
Every poem is an epic
Each novella is a novel
Well if life's a search for meaning
I think mine might have arrived
For now my life has a narrative arc –
because I almost died!

---

[20] ...And *three* godawful dad jokes per show!

Each example is a paragon
Each mini milk's a Feast
Every stroll's a London marathon
Now the acute abdominal pain has ceased.
There's a meal in every morsel -
in each crisp, a whole potater -
I feel practically immortal!
Due to my implantable cardioverter defibrillator.

Sure, some days I feel like an old man
but I'm still too young to die,
I've been through the slough of despond,
and come out the other side.
When things got tough, I'd once feel low,
hold thoughts of suicide –
but now I never shall, I know,
...because I almost died.

Every pasty is a Ginster's!
Every heckler's a mere wag!
Every frog's a princess!
Every car's a jag!
Now every dwarf's a BFG
Each burglar's a loveable rogue
Each Summer love's Eurydice
each tramp's ...that bloke out the Pogues?

Every mountain is a molehill
Every puddle is a loch
every sunset makes my soul thrill
every ham slice is a chop
Now CSI seems like The Wire
Each B-movie's Citizen Kane
Each damp squib's a roaring fire,
Every mullet is a mane
And even if I lose my breath
Each gasp's a laugh in the face of death
I'm crap at chess, but death's in check
Because I'm still alive.

Yes, If words were bullets I'd be a gatling gun
If hopes were bees I'd keep a hive
Though now it's time I stopped prattling on
about how I almost died,
because a lot of people
who've been in my position
...have.

*Ideally, exit the room to Pearl Jam's 'Alive' (edited to fade straight into
the chorus?)*

Billy Ray Cyrus's 'Achy breaky heart,' if feeling sadistic,

or Phil Collins's 'Two Hearts', if feeling masochistic.

Complications

I ♥ Roma

For James McKay.

How can a nation so cynical be so romantic with it?
Its Euros mint Venus, on the verso, Berlusconi;
Perhaps surfeit of love, frustrated, flips into cynicism.
I fall into step with two teenagers, girl guiding boy, scarf-blindfolded
through casual protests and orangery to the Aventine viewpoint.
He feigns awe. The sun, coin in a fountain, sinks beneath other lovers,
a German photographer, and someone pushing an invalid.
Which somehow makes me feel less alone.

Atop the Spanish Steps, near where Keats died, you see for miles.
A ghost skein of starlings twists across the sky, transforming,
dancing a discarded veil, skull, jellyfish, mushroom,
briefly, a heart. Bangladeshis prowl holding €1 roses and fixed smiles.
They cake whole districts in white shit, apparently, and the rich
hire special squads to scare them off with loud noises and guns.
The starlings, I mean, not the Bangladeshis - one of whom
finally sells three to a bloke whose wife must fish for cash in *her* purse.

I held court in the hostel dining room, dispensing shots like honours.
A girl slunk in behind dark curls and Il Figaro. I thought 'hell-o,'
waited an interval. She was Erasmus, I guessed Oxford: Cambridge.
Not mine, but not one of the arsehole colleges either. As for school,
I joked 'Cheltenham Ladies' College.' She was gobsmacked.
So I was psychic, her third year, languages. We talked of Comorra.
She translated stuff. I explained some Emperors. One of those instant
friendships forged only in squats, sinking ships and ostellos.

Next day we hit the Vatican. She'd a fancy to take communion.
We raced under starling bombers on shite-iced Via di Panico.
While I was scared that in my body, an Atheist Anglican,
the Eucharist would turn to poison, she happily dozed,
dividing my attention between Bernini's altar, her rosy cheekbones,
and the echoing Latin drone. I almost forgot to swallow, joked
'We're turning into Catholics now!' We talked pomp. Dad
had been Governor of Barbados. Sword, waiter's suit, feathered hat.

Her artist Mum once worked for Aid for Afghanistan. Had to say it:
'bet she met Bin Laden when he was a good guy,' guessed: Intelligence.
We hiked up to the Vatican cupola, covered in strange mosaics.
She said she'd like her bathroom like that. I sensed
'talking interior design already, could be wife material.'
Leaning cramped up the dome, concerned how hard my heart thumped.
'I can't feel this much already. Ha. Must just be claustrophobic.'
To free my mind from those clagged tunnels, I dusted off a character

Who'd last done service in Venice, another girl, another life.
Fastidious and boring, he sold those plastic treads that keep your grip.
'Did you know, there's over 2km of Steptreads™ in St Peter's over 351
                                                                    steps?
High quality polyethylene blend.' His name came from a warning sign.
'Bez, Bez Windy. Steptreads™ inc.' Their Corporate rivals, Treadsteps,
made exactly the same thing. 'I have the contract for all of the Vatican,
Treadsteps have all Jerusalem. But I will take it from them!'
She was cracking up. I was in luck: her ex had also been a comedian.

The summit crushed us, like angels slowly revolving on a pinhead.
She held my hand. I let myself imagine us as a retired couple.
On the roof below, we chatted like old friends, watched the sunset.
It could have been, were it not for the ten years that separated us,
ten years, and a class system older than the edifice we'd just scaled.
We ate Zabaglione. I showed her your favourite, turtle trapeze, fountain.
She skipped, girl-like, singing 'La Donna Mobile' near the Pantheon.
Perhaps she just missed being near an older man. Still, we held hands.

Next night the markets. She haggled for earrings. We ate gelatti,
laughed at a vast polony. The Kiwi girl went back early.
Tired, or she didn't like gooseberry flavour. We drank red
on a statue 'cos she claimed she was skint. Then she pointed
out a window in an Embassy palazzo where her Dad had once taken
her and her sister to a Reception. 'I remember now, they had
dancing, grand formal gardens, Roman ruins in the basement...'
She let me into that magical childhood before she lost him,

I made some crack about Ferrero Rocher
and dragged her to the arse-end of a poetry evening.
Never mind slam, all Italian speech is performance;
sound and dance. They always translate for the deaf with their hands.
I explained my theory of pan bi-sexuality over chocolate and Amaretto.
We found bad poetry in the night round Isola Tiberina; scoffed
at the pipistrelle colonies of teens' initialed, arrow-hearted locks.
Meant to last forever, just prey for bolt-cutters. She grimaced for a
                                                                    photo.

Crawling down to the Ponte's pillars and raging sluices,
I knew my heart beat too fast in relation to the danger.
'You can't die in the Tiber,' I joked nervously, 'unless you're a traitor.'
Crawling behind a pillar, for long seconds, she was with Schroedinger:
Emerged. I breathed. She translated plaques, we mutually rubbed backs,
then both got caught short in the ghetto, nipped down alleys for a slash.
The Bangladeshis tried to sell *us* a rose. She refused it.
But when I hugged her goodnight it was a small, still, only slightly-
                                                    awkward moment.

I inevitably messed it all up by trying to kiss her in the lift.
In the morning, she had to shop for a dictionary,
fly home. The rest's post-script. Me trudging, adrift,
through the labyrinth of the Vatican museums. In the Sistine
she texted, insisting she wished she could explore it with me.
Guards hissed 'Ssh! No foto!' 'But... I've a photographic memory!'
protested Bez Windy, wittily, but with no-one there to hear him.
On the Spanish steps, alone, no Bangladeshis drew near him.

So when Bez and I returned home, and she failed to return
our email, I sighed, unsurprised. But then, it wasn't just her
hand I'd been holding. It was that other girl's, ten years ago,
different time, *citta*, college, but me the same lewd old arsehole.
Look, if I count the ways my Muses are/aren't one, I'll get in trouble.
It's as complicated and longwinded as one of my essays,
let's just say: my love's as layered as Rome's living rubble.
It wasn't her broke my heart, but all of my histories.

Pain don't hurt

'Do you enjoy pain?' - Doc Clay
'Pain don't hurt.' - Dalton
Roadhouse, 1989

Age doesn't matter / **I'm no worse** / **Drugs make me better** / **Pain don't hurt** / Work's fulfilling / Haven't aged a day / He had it coming / You'd do the same / Course Santa reads it / Lost my phone / Our little secret / You're not alone / Dogs go to heaven / Cliff's not queer / Let's move to Devon / Couldn't happen here / **I'll quit tomorrow** / **Kilts aren't skirts** / **The blues ain't sorrow** / **Pain don't hurt**

You're not stupid! / Just this once / He's not worth it! / Keep in touch / Have no fear / Thirty's not old / Buck stops here / Don't feel cold / We're not hiring / Call me Dad / God's just hiding / Yes, we can! / **It's not infected** / **Talking works** / **Honestly detective** / **Pain don't hurt**

Course we'll miss you / Shit don't stink / Race's not an issue / Daddy doesn't drink / We're still together / Hearts will mend / Things'll get better / Still be friends? / Love is the answer / Death's not the end / Cure for cancer / Time – mends **Change in the weather** / **Love's no curse** / **In this together** / **Pain don't hurt**

Age doesn't matter / **I'm no worse** / **Keeping it together** / **Pain don't hurt**

...but sometimes, you get what you need.

After Heather Holden

You want William Shakespeare, you get William Shatner.
You want to explore new worlds, you get hooked on Second Life.
You want spiritual guidance, you get satnav voiced by Uri Geller.
You want a girlfriend experience, you get your second wife.

You want Prince Charming, you get the Prince of Wales.
You want a mobile home, you get snails.
You want a sign from God, you get a visit from the Jehovah's
                                                    Witnesses.
You want your kids to do better than you. They become
                                                    Conservatives.

We eat in the car and call it a picnic

You want fine writing, you get strong language.
You want to catch a falling star, you get flying ants.
You want a feast fit for an Earl, you grab a sandwich.
You want Laphroaig, you get Grants.

You want air miles, you get exile,
You want a quiet night in, you get a curfew,
You want to experience foreign cultures, you get invaded,
You want self-sufficiency, you get blockaded.

Staying till closing time, that's a night out

You want The Beatles, you get Oasis.
You want Anne Boleyn, you get Anne of Cleves.
You want life to be like Wacky Races, you just meet wacky racists.
You want Handel's Messiah, you get Greensleeves.

You want Home Ownership, you get homeopathy.
You're want a nice cardie, you get cardiomyopathy.
You want a wake-up call, you get a fire alarm,
You want to move to the country, you almost buy the farm.

We settle for cuddles and call it a marriage

You want the Simpsons, you get the Jetsons.
You want a rainbow, you get a prism.
You want an heir, you get a stepson.
You want time to think, you get prison.

You want when Harry met Sally, you get Paul & Barry.
You want Johnny Cash, you get cash & carry.
You want to make a difference, you barely make a living.
You want whatever she's having, you get what you're given.

We lie in bed crying, we're working from home.

All your ex-girlfriends as Soviet statue park

The first has been decapitated. Her eyes severe, colour gone,
could stare out seas or deserts, but instead gaze over a sliproad
to the retail park. This one's legs, which your current squeeze
poses inbetween for a photo, digital, not polaroid,
are still shapely despite the mould. That one's almost still whole,
I think she holds a discus, or is it chips? She's too far away. That one,
the short one, her pointing wrist now buried in the ground holds up
just her head and torso, like a broken breakdancer. The one with a
bob
hefts a thick book, longingly surveys a flat on the run-down blocks.
Drizzle hunts your eye from some far-up granite rill.
The martial one looks up and out for planes, will never meet your gaze,
and the one you always overlook is just an unsmiling bust. Strange,
what you must now pay to see what was once immanent.
Your current's in the gift shop, so your artistic eye can't size her up.
Suns set. Atoms swap. Their gazes of porphyry, basalt, pumice,
strain to recall what they saw in your lust.

Sky picnic

Everyone you know is inverted to the Sky Picnic,
please PRSV. It'll take place above the highest terrace
of the Greenbacks, above the Millibard tree, we'll have
clouds-on-toast, own brand Ferrero Rocher,
all the vol-au-vents the future has to offer.
(The woman with one face will be there)
Tech level: Some nudity. Drinks: Mild peril, Becks Zero.
The forcefield will stop all flies like bullets
and shoot them back at fate. The sun's booked,
all dogs' bums will be firmly plugged,
the rain will at most form a plaintive faraway singing
(the man from Del Mondrake will be there)
the pollen and the poetry are all non-allergenic
and calibrated, subject-and-metre, to attendees' biosignals.

It's a shame you must respectfully decline:
These days, you can fly anywhere but you can't *walk*.

NATO is my flatmate

He often misses the bowl.
He bought this far-too-sophisticated alarm
and somehow, we all ended up paying for it.
Still never been burgled, except that one time
he left the window open.
Still, we made the most of *that* insurance claim.

Serial monogamist, while still hitched
he'll scour dark bars for a new ex,
or pick on some short bloke in a quiet club,
smashing his neck before he can think
what the hell he's supposed to have done.
Man, especially after that French girl left.
One night he came back so pissed
he lay a depth-charge in the fish-tank.

Once, when caterpillars hatched
in his bag of economy porridge,
he kept it on the window ledge.
Chrysalises swung for a month
among the silk-spun oats,
but when they hatched as moths,
for a short time, he watched,
then shook them up, chucked them out.

But I know I'll never move. It's mate's rates,
we've seen those noisy neighbours off,
he's so attentively aggressively friendly,
and whatever else happens,
the cleaning rota gets maintained.
Besides, his uncle owns the whole block.

The day everybody in the World's arsehole disappeared

Everyone remembers what they were doing on the day everybody in the world's arsehole disappeared. They were, in general, checking to see if their arsehole had disappeared.

I found out through my role as a G.P. A patient of mine, Mr Patel, a hardworking middle-aged shop-keeper who I hardly saw and who had only dropped by because he'd been coughing up blood mentioned, in passing, after I'd told him I'd send his samples off for tests, that he thought he might be going mad.

'I really did not want to mention it Doctor, but I think I am having hallucinations. Today I think I am thinking that my anus has disappeared.'

Suspecting some language difficulty, I undertook to examine Mr Patel's posterior expecting to diagnose an abscess or piles, only to find that indeed his anus had vanished. There was no seam, nor scar, not a pockmark or indentation to mark where his rectum should have resided. I remained calm.

'I'm afraid, Mr Patel, that your arsehole does in fact seem to... not be in the expected position. How long has it been like this?'
'Since perhaps this morning. I noticed it in your toilet. I definitely had it last night though, because I...'
At that stage I should have called in my colleague Dr Chakraboty, or the nurse, but I really wasn't entirely sure that I wasn't hallucinating myself. To this date, I am still not. Instead I murmured 'Interesting,' and told Mr Patel to book another appointment on the way out.

Next, I carried out a few quick checks. First, I firmly pinched my left forearm to ensure I wasn't dreaming. Then, after a pause long enough only to decide that yes, to check my own arsehole would be ridiculous, I checked my own arsehole. Or rather, my lack of own arsehole. My anal cleft was as smooth and unyielding as Mr Patel's. Though less hairy. And less brown. My perineum formed an unbroken valley from my scrotal sac to my lumbar region; in short, I had no arsehole. I was suddenly taken with the urge to vomit – the first time I had felt that reflex sober since my first day at med school – but kept it down. Then, the thought that from now on, vomiting might prove the only way food waste could exit my body overcame my will. Special K leapt onto my brogues.

I suppose this is where my story enters the public domain, enters everybody else's. My arse comparison with Dr Chakraborty. Our scientific, disinterested interest. Nurse Oluboleweju's horror. The news broadcasts, the pundits. Everyone glued to screens, desperate for someone, anyone to answer the question of where and when and how their shit was going to come out. The slow realisation, dawning across the world, that no-one was in fact feeling the need to evacuate their bowels – 'Well you know something Judy, I'm not even feeling the need to do a – number two - right now, and I certainly think that by now I would be,' uttered Richard Madeley, sagely. The slow realisation, dawning across the world, that the question of how in God's name all of this was scientifically possible was ultimately intractable.

The pontification flowed so freely it seemed as if the media was trying to replace the waste that would no longer be provided by arseholes with surrogate faeces from the mouths and minds of hastily dredged-up experts. Even before it became obvious that a scientific explanation was impossible, the moral and allegorical ones had commenced. Some of the religious prayed for the return of their lost poop-chutes. Others thanked God for this punishment against homosexuals. On the Radio, Peter Tatchell was actually asked 'So how will you be gay now?' to which he replied 'og og og', miming fellatio. Geneticists suspected some kind of sudden leap of evolution but were at a loss to explain its mechanisms. Most people agreed that it had to be some kind of metaphor for something, but no-one could agree what. In the confusion, most wars screeched to a halt for at least two or three days.

By about 2pm, the joke texts had started – one about how Jake the Peg, the man with the extra leg, was especially upset at having lost both his two arseholes, another in which he was in fact the only man on Earth left in possession of a spare, police were looking into it, that sort of thing. My favourite stated how in the current spate of arsehole disappearances, Radio 1 DJ Chris Moyles had vanished completely off the face of the Earth. The psychiatry component of my G.P. training taught me that use of humour was the best indication that someone was beginning to accept a traumatic situation; so I found such missives reassuring rather than sick.

The Day Everybody in the World's Arsehole Disappeared was not of course, its official label – though now we mainly refer to the occurrence by its date, there were many names accorded it – 'no arse day', V-A day; some cruel and waggish internet pundits even referred to it as the 'Anal Holocaust'.

From there on in of course bums started to be no longer seen as such sexualised areas and they're now mainly used just for sitting, and though they're still obviously the part of the body best-adapted for spanking, that activity really doesn't have the edge it once did. When one views pornographic footage of anal sex now, it seems incredibly historical, wistful, like watching a black and white movie and remarking to yourself 'that kitten is dead, that woman is dead, that shopkeeper is dead.' Those who have had their arseholes surgically remade know full well they don't connect to anything, and that the healing gashes in their rear ends are a pale imitation of their former mouse airlocks.

Of course, there have now been two, three generations of human beings born with no experience of arseholes at all – which is why, for what it's worth, I now endeavour to set down my experiences for posterity. I am late to this; at the time, for weeks school-rooms and open-mics around the world resonated with the sounds of 'arse trauma-therapy-lit.' For soon toilet tissue, fart gags, suppositories, bumming, rimming, diarrhoea, lucky shits, the very concept of dung itself - all shall pass out of living memory; into the annals of History. And while we lived in fear, for a while, that nipples, penises, vaginas or testes might be next, our fears have so far proved unfounded – though we must now wonder what other mucous orifices, prehensile appendages or putative third eyes lie sloughed, unmarked by paper trail or fossil record, in the dark forgotten catacombs of human evolution. There is still much navel-gazing to be done.

It's my funeral

for Young Dawkins

It's hard, when a friend's already poemed their own funeral,
to out-do them. You really have to push the longboat out
For although no-one can truly imagine their own death,
your executors may feel obliged to at least attempt what you think up.
Given that:

I want go-go dancers. Not just evening class, middle-class
'burlesque artistes' with titty twisters like velour curtain tassles
but the pre-post-modern, real thing. Go-go dancers
dancing on my grave with more go-go than Inspector Gadget.

There will be a twenty-tiered wedding cake
but instead of a couple on top of the wedding cake
there'll just be me in a marzipan coffin
and the icing sugar will be BLACK. On it,
I want the local primary to make a papier-mache vignette
of all the levels of the Inferno and its different punishments
and it's me in every one giving a thumbs-up Doré duck face
to Dante & John Virgo

It's harder when Bentham's already done 'boxed' - you must do better
so turn me into a plasticised corpse that jigs to a tinkly drumstep tune
and gives you a plastic-egged prize when you insert 50p for charities
like a seaside Lenin in King's College Chapel foyer.

Now, music. A massive rave playing horrible clumpcore
that I'd never get anyone to come with me to if I were alive
but now I'm dead they all feel emotionally blackmailed into it and do,
so even my ex, yes the real one, hangs round for almost an hour.

I want bass to quake your bowels so loud you must empty them
before you hit the dancefloor. Then you can eat more swan-au-vents.
Invite all the people that hated me and are glad I'm dead
for at least those bastards will dance,
and half the time I agreed with them,
and forgiveness is often the best possible insult.

It's hardest when you've actually already held your own funeral -
I mean what if less people turn up to your real one?
You really have to go absolutely stiffing crazy
its a strain on both imagination and humility
like trying to crap a breezeblock of hubris
through the centre of a party ring.
Don't forget the party rings.

Burn down the house of Utter!
Stop all the atomic clocks
Prevent a dog from anything with a whole mammoth skeleton
Smash legoland to build me a pyramid-sized pyramid
Burn London
Rush out an unauthorised biography like it was already waiting
Have my authorised paint me as a bigger cad than the unauthorised
Get all my children to play me in the film of my life
Burn the sun

I will live on in your dreams
I will live on in your hangovers
I will live on in your tribute poems
But your tribute poems will never be as good as this one,
For none of you knew me like I did.
But please, please yourself. Insist
'it's what he would have wanted',
knowing I'll never know.

Footprints in the sand

One night I dreamed I was walking along the beach with the Lord. Many scenes from my life flashed across the sky.

In each scene I noticed footprints in the sand. Sometimes there were two sets of footprints, other times there was only one.

This bothered me because I noticed that, during the low periods of my life, when I was suffering from pain, anguish or defeat, I could see only one set of footprints. So I said to the Lord,

"You promised me Lord, that if I followed you, you would walk with me always. But I have noticed that during the hardest, most trying periods of my life there has been only one set of footprints in the sand. Why Lord, when I needed you most, did you abandon me?"

The Lord replied, "Oh my son, but at those hardest, most trying times of your life... you were being an annoying, self-pitying, sniveling little shit. Can you blame me for fucking off?"

"Yeah, fair enough Lord," I agreed.